31-Day Christian Devotional

ANEW
Spiritual
Awakening

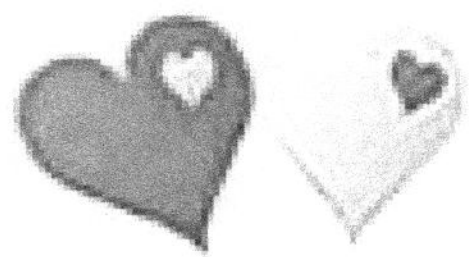

*Let God's Love
Transform Life's Brokenness
Into Something Beautiful*

J. V. Lauren, P.E.

Copyright © 2020 by J. V. Lauren, P.E.

Published by ABC Financial Pro, Inc. Torrance, California, USA

ANEW Spiritual Awakening: 31-Day Christian Devotional, Let God's Love Transform Life's Brokenness Into Something Beautiful

ISBN: 978-1-63732-917-7 ebook

978-1-63732-918-4 paperback

FIRST EDITION

DEDICATION

This daily Christian devotional is dedicated to my late son, who is my angel with wings, and my twin boys, who are my angels with feet.

"Jesus looked at them and said, 'With man this is impossible, but with God all things are possible'" (Matthew 19:26, New International Version Bible).

❤ FREE GIFTS

Download your FREE PDF copies of the ANEW posters at www.anewwaynow.com!

ANEW Spiritual Awakening I AM ANEW Poster from A to Z has been created to keep you motivated throughout the month.

ANEW Spiritual Awakening BLANK I AM ANEW Poster from A to Z has been created so you can rewrite the transformations in this devotional each day or add your own.

Table of Contents

❤ ♡ **INTRODUCTION**

"Therefore, if anyone is in Christ, he is a new creation; the old has gone, the new has come!" (2 Corinthians 5:17, New International Version Bible).

<u>Would you like to be made ANEW?</u> Imagine that you are already loveable and worthy of God's love. Believe that each thought, feeling, trait, attribute, and experience, each feature of your life, can be used for good. God wants to heal the brokenness of your life into something beautiful. Can you see it, feel it, and believe it? Let it sink in; it's true. God is always bigger than our challenges. His power and love can make us ANEW. Life is a paradox only God can transform. From clouds to rainbows, valleys to mountaintops, darkness to light, and brokenness to beauty, God's hands constantly shape us.

As believers, we know Jesus came to let the world know we are His precious children. In the Bible, Jesus and Paul instruct us to put off the old, broken self and put on the new, beautiful self in God. Yet, how do we do that? *ANEW Spiritual Awakening: 31-Day Christian Devotional, Companion Journal: 31-Day Christian Workbook,* the I AM ANEW poster, and the Blank I AM ANEW poster offer an answer. Use these four resources together to stay on track each day and for a deeper transformation.

You can find the *ANEW Spiritual Awakening: Companion Journal* at https://www.amazon.com/dp/B08PFZ1DND. The ANEW Posters are FREE to view, print, or download at www.anewwaynow.com.

<u>Who is served by this daily devotional?</u> It's for those who want to feel the transformative power of God's love in a broken world. It's for those who struggle with perfectionism or negativity. It's for those who've experienced abuse, neglect, addiction, alcoholism, trauma, mental illness, or chaos in their families or their lives. It's for those inside and outside of the church and self-help communities, who want a closer walk with Jesus.

<u>How does this daily devotional work?</u> This thirty-one-day devotional and companion journal guide the reader on a daily transformation process in as little as ten minutes a day. Each devotion focuses on one or an equal number of life's beautiful and broken features from A to Z. The daily devotions include short narratives, prayers, meditations, quotes, reflections, and scriptures from the New International Version Bible unless otherwise noted. There is an action section each day to take a daily balanced personal inventory, as explained below.

<u>What is a personal inventory?</u> In the Bible and self-help communities, a personal inventory is a process of offering up my brokenness to take on the beautiful likeness of God. Jesus explains, *"If any of you wants to be my follower, you must give up your own way, take up your cross daily, and follow me" (Luke 9:23 New Living Translation).* In Romans 8:28-9, Paul expands on this guidance, *"And we know that in all things God works for the good of those who love him, who have been called according to his purpose. For those God foreknew he also predestined to be conformed to the likeness of his Son."*

In simpler terms, a personal inventory is akin to a grocer, who takes stock of a store. The manager catalogs each product and then goes to the next one. The broken and expired products will get discarded and replaced with new ones. The process will be repeated for each shelf. A personal inventory takes stock of the broken and beautiful features of our lives.

<u>What do you mean by the terms "broken" and "beautiful" features?</u> The definitions are:

- **Broken Features**: These are the unpleasant parts of life, including the traits, attributes, thoughts, feelings, aspects, and experiences for God to decrease and transform.

- **Beautiful Features**: These are the pleasant parts of life, including the traits, attributes, thoughts, feelings, aspects, and experiences for God to enhance.

Up until now, we have tried to transform life's brokenness in our power; from now on we call upon God's power.

<u>What to journal each day?</u> Each day after reading this devotional, there is a take action section to connect this book to ANEW's companion journal or you can use a personal notebook. Reflect on these questions each day:

- Ask God to transform life's brokenness into something beautiful each day, remembering this truth, "I am a beloved child of God."
- Write or draw your thoughts, feelings, and memories about the broken and beautiful features presented.
- Create an action plan for whom, when, and how to apologize, make amends, change your behavior, and offer forgiveness including to yourself.
- Take time to pray and meditate on the daily devotion, scriptures, prayers, and your action steps.
- Go deeper by reflecting on other features, balancing in equal number the broken and beautiful parts of your life.

<u>Disclaimer:</u> This devotional will take some work. As you go through it, a myriad of thoughts and feelings will likely come up, which may or may not feel like a spiritual awakening. It will take time and effort to work through them and move beyond them with God's help. You are encouraged to continue to give your thoughts and feelings to God. Lastly, this devotional does not guarantee a spiritual awakening, as that is a God-sized job.

<u>These are my prayers for you</u>. May *ANEW Spiritual Awakening: 31-Day Christian Devotional* be a blessing to you. I pray you come to believe in a loving Higher Power revealed in Jesus Christ. *"If you declare with your mouth, 'Jesus is Lord,' and believe in your heart that God raised him from the dead, you will be saved" (Romans 10:9).* Imagine running to God with the assurance that He is running with open arms towards you.

My grandmother always said, "Put your left hand on your right shoulder; put your right hand on your left shoulder; and, give yourself a big hug from me. Can you feel it?" I imagine that God embraces each of us this way, and I offer this same hug to you. Consider holding your devotional in this same way.

<u>A special note for readers in self-help communities</u>. You don't need to be in a Twelve Step program to use this devotional. However, if you are, this book is not meant to replace your program material. Please discuss with your sponsor about using this book's framework as an adjunct to your program. It shares my experience, strength, and hope from Twelve Step recovery and the love of God in Christ.

CHAPTER 1 – A FEATURES
Anger to Acceptance

Dear God, thank You that I am transformed and made ANEW from the broken feature of ANGER with the beautiful feature of ACCEPTANCE by You.

Anger is a powerful emotion, yet emotions aren't bad. They are not defective. Emotions are just feelings. I've learned that it is how I act on or judge my feelings that can be negative. Righteous anger that causes me to take action to correct injustice is valuable. Passion is a great motivator. Jesus was angry but did not sin when he turned over the tables in the temple because he was standing up for God and the temple.

When I was a kid, however, I was bitter and resentful, and they hurt me. Why was my mom an alcoholic? Why were my parents divorced? I had to play grown-up when I wanted to be a kid. It didn't feel right or fair. These toxic forms of anger are seductive; they poison the vessel that contains them. When I let small hurts, irritations, and frustrations build, they can give rise to bitterness, resentments, and eventually wrath. If I'm holding onto poison, then I get sick from its venom.

Frustrations are often at the root of destructive anger. Unmet expectations, taking responsibility for other people, and disrespect breed frustrations. If my expectations are based on other people not respecting my boundaries, I first ought to ask myself if I communicated them and if I'm respecting them myself. If I keep playing ball with someone who doesn't respect my boundaries, I'm not honoring myself. In essence, I am volunteering for my misery. I don't need to volunteer anymore for relationships and situations that lead to anger.

Something to Think About

At the root of frustrations, bitterness, and resentments was my lack of acceptance that life isn't fair. It took time to realize that my parents, family, friends, and myself are perfectly, imperfect human beings doing the best we can at any given moment.

My power came from radically accepting my powerlessness and connecting to the unlimited power of God. My acceptance of life exactly as it is and people exactly as they are, transforms me. I also came to understand that my loved ones may not be capable of being who or what I need or want them to be. The moment I allow life to be as it is without my interference or meddling to change it, that's when the Holy Spirit starts to change my attitudes and my life. I get to release destructive anger by accepting and forgiving myself and others for being who we are.

My sponsor often tells me to feel my feelings, move through them, then be gentle with myself. Could it be that the very things that make me angry are the things that God wants me to accept? People are likely to upset and hurt me unintentionally and intentionally. They won't measure up to my standards and expectations. Sometimes I don't even measure up to myself.

The Father loves and accepts each of us just as we are, and that's why He sent His Son, Jesus Christ. This precious gift from the Lord inspires me to love and be gentle with myself and others. We are loved by Him and belong, just as we are.

Quote to Ponder

"Get rid of all bitterness, rage and anger, brawling and slander, along with every form of malice. Be kind and compassionate to one another, forgiving each other, just as in Christ God forgave you" (Ephesians 4:31-2).

Take Action

Write, draw, pray, meditate, and reflect in ANEW's companion journal as follows:

Broken Feature:	Beautiful Feature:
Dear God, thank You for transforming the broken feature of ANGER into something beautiful.	Dear God, thank You for transforming the beautiful feature of ACCEPTANCE into something even more beautiful.

Questions beyond the introductory suggestions

- When do I first remember getting angry?
- Was anger allowed or were feelings shamed in my childhood? Is it allowed now in my home?
- What are some challenging experiences in my life that I have accepted by letting go and letting God be in charge?
- What perpetually happens that continues to frustrate me and leads to anger instead of acceptance?

💗 💕 CHAPTER 2 – B FEATURES
Betrayal to Benevolence

Dear God, thank You that I am transformed and made ANEW from the broken feature of BETRAYAL with the beautiful feature of BENEVOLENCE by You.

It is a struggle to be benevolent towards those who have betrayed me and my trust. My first betrayals were abandonment and neglect from my childhood. I had childlike expectations from my innocence that the world and my mother were meant to be good and to protect me. Instead, I grew up believing the words of others over their actions.

My childhood betrayals resulted in many years of getting hurt, neglected, and abused, including sexual abuse. I kept believing my mother and other people would change. I hoped that people would be different than they are and wanted to believe that the world was going to be something different than it was. Life doesn't often work that way.

You, like I, may have experienced betrayals in the forms of injuries, abuses, or traumas in the past or you may have been the victim of a terrible crime. It is easy to take on a victim or martyr identity when I have not received an apology or amends for the pain that I've experienced. It is challenging for me to let go of hurt towards people who have betrayed me.

When I say yes, but I mean no, I betray myself. At work, home, or in life, playing the hero or the martyr is considered praiseworthy. *Jesus said, "All you need to say is simply 'Yes' or 'No'" (Matthew 5:37).* Having healthy boundaries and just saying "no" are ways to gently embrace my authentic self.

When I got to the end of the martyr or victim rope, this was when I reached out for help from God and others. I remember to seek God's benevolence and loving communities.

Something to Think About

Can the troubles of the past make life better? Yes! I get to stop betraying myself. I get to look on the inside rather than the outside. God is the benevolent force that transforms the betrayals I've experienced into something beautiful.

The root of betrayal is attachment to pain from the past and the expectation that life should have been different than it was. When I let the Holy Spirit be my guide, I am more able to transform the years of feeling betrayed by life and others. I cannot do this in my power, but from God's power that is moving through me.

Remembering that life is a continual process of becoming better over time helps me realize that God is still working on me and others with His benevolence. When I let go of past betrayals, I become charitable with myself and others.

Quote to Ponder

"Do not be overcome by evil, but overcome evil with good" (Romans 12:21).

Take Action

Write, draw, pray, meditate, and reflect in ANEW's companion journal as follows:

Broken Feature:	Beautiful Feature:
Dear God, thank You for transforming the broken feature of BETRAYAL into something beautiful.	Dear God, thank You for transforming the beautiful feature of BENEVOLENCE into something even more beautiful.

Questions beyond the introductory suggestions

- Can I remember the first time and the last time I felt betrayed? What happened?
- Have I learned that when someone betrays or abuses me that it is not my fault?
- Am I ready to let myself off the hook for not having known better at the time when I was betrayed and show myself gentleness?
- How can I show benevolence to my current and former self?

❤️ **CHAPTER 3 – C FEATURES**
Criticism to Compassion

Dear God, thank You that I am transformed and made ANEW from the broken feature of CRITICISM with the beautiful feature of COMPASSION by You.

Many words have more than one meaning. To be critical or analytical of things is useful in business. However, criticism or speaking disparagingly of people, including myself, can be hurtful. Sometimes my workplace behaviors are not beneficial in relationships.

As an engineer criticism was valuable. We fixed things at work. However, constructive feedback for others, even if positive, can feel like hurtful criticism. I thought I was helping, but I wasn't. Advice, especially when it's unsolicited, is often an attempt to fix others. It keeps people from experiencing the dignity of handling their affairs on their own with God's help. My impatient responses lack compassion and can block others from the prompting of the Holy Spirit.

I found that most people in Christian and self-help communities are everyday people who struggle with life and relationships. We want to feel enough and worthy of God's love. When I remember to speak lovingly towards myself and other people, things go smoothly in my relationships. Yet, when I feel strongly that doom is going to befall them without my protection, it's time for me to spend time with God and be gentle with myself.

It can be challenging to be compassionate with myself and others. I remember that we are loved by God as works in progress. It's not my job to fix others; that's God's job.

Something to Think About

It's easy to get sucked into overanalyzing. I can be my worst critic, which often leads me to be critical of others. Self-criticism leads to believing that I'm unworthy of God's love, forgiveness, and blessings. Soon, I lose my connection with the Holy Spirit. Yet, gentleness begins when I stop beating myself up, get up, and run to God, only to see Him running to me.

When I show compassion towards myself for being human, I get to extend that to others. The entire picture of anyone's life, including my own, is best seen by the Lord. Humility allows His plan to be revealed in my life and the lives of others.

It is when I deserve compassion least, that is when I need it the most. The same goes for others. Sometimes an offering of a listening ear or a hug speaks louder than spoken words.

Let me remember to close my mouth and open my heart and arms to God and others. I get to give myself and others the grace to find each of our paths to Jesus. If God is about to move mountains, I ought to get out of His way.

Quote to Ponder

"So [the lost son] got up and went to his father. But while he was still a long way off, his father saw him and was filled with compassion for him; he ran to his son, threw his arms around him and kissed him" (Luke 15:20).

Take Action

Write, draw, pray, meditate, and reflect in ANEW's companion journal as follows:

Broken Feature:	Beautiful Feature:
Dear God, thank You for transforming the broken feature of CRITICISM into something beautiful.	Dear God, thank You for transforming the beautiful feature of COMPASSION into something even more beautiful.

Questions beyond the introductory suggestions

- Do I think I know what is best for other people? Can I leave them to their walk with the Lord?
- How long does it take me to analyze a situation before I make a decision or do I get sucked into overanalyzing?
- Can I give myself and other people a break for being human?
- In what areas of my life do I need to remove criticism and add compassion?

❤ 🤍 CHAPTER 4 – D FEATURES
Distracted to Disciplined

Dear God, thank You that I am transformed and made ANEW from the broken feature of DISTRACTED with the beautiful feature of DISCIPLINED by You.

I can be lazy. I want the benefits of having a spiritual awakening without having to do what I ought to do to maintain my relationship with the Lord. I forget, get distracted, and soon I've wandered away from God's will.

When I fill my body with junk food and my mind with negativity, I can get physically, spiritually, and emotionally sick. If I put garbage in, I get garbage out. I also struggle to take care of myself.

Many times, I've put aside my needs to take care of other people. Throughout my life, I was giving water from my cup to others, which left me thirsty. Now, I can remember to ask myself, "Is my cup running over to give to others, or is it empty?" If it's empty, I need only go to Jesus to get filled up.

If I want to be useful to God and others, I ought to discipline myself to take care of my connection with the Holy Spirit first each day. This discipline leads to self-control and perseverance, as well as giving from my abundance.

Jesus is big enough for me to lean on him. He gives me the courage to set boundaries with others, discipline myself, and make time for my needs. This in turn leads me to prioritize learning and making healthy choices. Each day I choose to set time aside to pray and meditate on God's will for my life so He can transform each broken feature one day at a time.

Something to Think About

As a Civil Engineering student, I used to say, "Why put off until tomorrow what I can get out of entirely?" It's a funny saying, but it was a great way to prioritize, delegate, and discipline myself to get more done. However, at times it also led to procrastination and distraction. Now that I'm an adult, I recognize that I still spend parts of my day on distractions rather than seeking God's will for my life.

My hopes, dreams, and changes can be found in Christ alone. I can be found by God when I am disciplined enough to put Jesus first. *"No discipline seems pleasant at the time, but painful. Later on, however, it produces a harvest of righteousness and peace for those who have been trained by it" (Hebrews 12:11).*

The best way that I've found to keep the hope of joy and freedom alive in my life is through discipline. I start each day by praying and meditating on God's love, forgiveness, will, and plan for my life.

Quote to Ponder

"I realize I am not You, God. I've often tried to control my problems, my pain, my image, and even other people—as if I were You. I'm sorry. I've tried to deny my problems by staying busy and keeping distracted. But I'm not running anymore" (Baker 2007, p. 23).

Take Action

Write, draw, pray, meditate, and reflect in ANEW's companion journal as follows:

Broken Feature:	Beautiful Feature:
Dear God, thank You for transforming the broken feature of DISTRACTED into something beautiful.	Dear God, thank You for transforming the beautiful feature of DISCIPLINED into something even more beautiful.

Questions beyond the introductory suggestions

- What do I do, day after day, that keeps me distracted?
- In what areas of my life have I been putting off until tomorrow what needed to get done yesterday? Today?
- How can I lean upon the Holy Spirit to guide me to what I can do to be more disciplined in my life?
- How can I be less distracted and more disciplined with my time, priorities, relationships, home, health, work, passions, etc.?

❤ 🤍 CHAPTER 5 – E FEATURES
Envy to Empathy

Dear God, thank You that I am transformed and made ANEW from the broken feature of ENVY with the beautiful feature of EMPATHY by You.

Why does he get the breaks? Why does she look glamorous in the clothes she wears? Why does that family have so much fun? When I compare my insides to other people's outside, I feel envy. When I think in such extremes, I elevate people, things, and situations above God. People are human beings, and thus imperfect. People's dispositions and circumstances may seem happy on the surface, but how can I know their hearts? Their smile may be covering up unhappiness, burdens, or pain.

I am limited by envy through dissatisfaction and continually desiring and comparing myself to what others have, whether it is status, abilities, possessions, spouse, friends, work, money, etc. If someone has what I want, then I ask God to show me the plan for me alone. It may or may not include what I desire.

When I feel envy, I dehumanize myself and others. I ought to remember that I am a precious child of God and to see the same in others. I can gain empathy for myself and others when I seek to understand what others are experiencing internally and stop comparing my insides with others' outsides.

I can start by being vulnerable with my pain and darkness. Then I show empathy to others when I allow them to share their pain and sadness with me. Jesus did this when Lazarus died. Jesus empathized with Martha and Mary with the shortest Bible verse, which is *John 11:35: "Jesus wept."*

Something to Think About

To have a friend, I ought to be a friend. That means showing encouragement and empathy towards others. It is not enough to imagine walking a mile in someone else's shoes; I can best empathize with another if I can imagine being that person and walking a mile in his or her shoes.

If I play the martyr or the victim by envying other people, I have put them on a pedestal, thinking their lives are perfect. This thinking blocks me from authentic relationships with myself and others.

I desire real people in my life, not empty idols. Real people experience real joy and sorrow, as well as real successes and failures. Today, let me empathize with the real struggles that other people are going through, rejoice in their achievements, and offer comfort for the challenges they are facing. By letting go of envy, I get to give up self-pity and give myself some empathy for my journey and the journeys of others.

Quote to Ponder

"Let us not become conceited, provoking and envying each other" (Galatians 5:26).

Take Action

Write, draw, pray, meditate, and reflect in ANEW's companion journal as follows:

Broken Feature:	Beautiful Feature:
Dear God, thank You for transforming the broken feature of ENVY into something beautiful.	Dear God, thank You for transforming the beautiful feature of EMPATHY into something even more beautiful.

Questions beyond the introductory suggestions

- Do I compare my insides with other peoples' outsides and feel envy for them?
- Can I accept that I cannot know what is happening in someone else's life beyond the surface?
- How can I show empathy for myself, my story, and the challenges I've experienced in my life?
- What questions can I ask myself and others so I sow seeds of empathy rather than seeds of envy?

❤ CHAPTER 6 – F FEATURES
Fearful to Forgiveness

Dear God, thank You that I am transformed and made ANEW from the broken feature of FEARFUL with the beautiful feature of FORGIVENESS by You.

Growing up, I felt fearful that I could not be forgiven. I was running away from what I thought was a scary god, but now I run to the Lord. Fear is a feeling. Faith is a choice, and forgiveness is its byproduct. When by faith, I surrender to the love, the will, and the forgiveness of God in Christ, I conquer fear. *"There is no fear in love. But perfect love drives out fear, because fear has to do with punishment. The one who fears is not made perfect in love"* *(1 John 4:18).*

Fear is rooted in pride, but faith and forgiveness are rooted in trust. God is trustworthy. He eases my anxious heart when I recognize that He loves and forgives me completely. That is why He sent Jesus, and to show us how to love and forgive ourselves and others. The love and forgiveness from the Holy Spirit overflow from me to others.

It can be challenging to trust when I feel scared or that I might fail. I want immediate relief from my fear and become impatient with the Lord's timing, will, and plans. Often instead of waiting, I meddle with His plans by injecting my own, often misguided, control. The results are often disastrous. When I decide to act out of fear, apart from God's will for my life and others' lives, these decisions often backfire.

I continue to believe that things work out for good for my loved ones and me. If I feel overwhelmed, I start by giving God the small stuff, then the larger stuff, and then my life itself. He fulfills my seemingly impossible tasks and dreams.

Something to Think About

By injecting forgiveness into memories of the past, I change the past. When I forgive my expectations of myself, people, and situations as being different than they were in the past, I forgive them for not being who I wanted or needed them to be.

When I accept the Lord's forgiveness for my past and put my faith in Him for my future, I receive freedom from fear. When I forgive others, I stop hurting myself; I stop letting people take up mind space without paying rent. I accept with faith that we each do the best we can, given our knowledge and emotions at that moment, and that is good enough.

It is humbling to realize that God is in control, not me. Surrendering my fears and accepting forgiveness allows me to let go of whatever situation is troubling me.

Quote to Ponder

"Then Peter came to Jesus and asked, 'Lord, how many times shall I forgive my brother [or sister who] sins against me? Up to seven times?' Jesus answered, 'I tell you, not seven times, but seventy-seven times" (Matthew 18:21-2).

Take Action

Write, draw, pray, meditate, and reflect in ANEW's companion journal as follows:

Broken Feature:	Beautiful Feature:
Dear God, thank You for transforming the broken feature of FEARFUL into something beautiful.	Dear God, thank You for transforming the beautiful feature of FORGIVENESS into something even more beautiful.

Questions beyond the introductory suggestions

- What were my biggest fears as a child? Am I still afraid of the same things?
- Do I believe that fear stands for "false evidence appearing real" and I ought to "face everything and rise?"
- Can I list the people, experiences, and parts of my life that I have not forgiven for fear of losing control?
- Will I consider that forgiving myself for believing life and people would be anything different than they are is freedom from fear?

CHAPTER 7 – REFLECTIONS
Features from A to F

Dear God, thank You that I am transformed and made ANEW from these A to F broken features with beautiful ones by You.

God is making me ANEW from A to F! Use this day to catch up, rest, and/or reflect on these questions in ANEW's companion journal:

- Are there any nagging thoughts or feelings I have, especially about anger and fear?
- What are some specific actions I can take to be more disciplined with my journaling, prayer, and meditation time each day?
- How can empathy for myself and others from my childhood to today release the pain of these broken features from A to F?

Quote to Ponder

"But you, Lord, are a compassionate and gracious God, slow to anger, abounding in love and faithfulness" (Psalm 86:15).

With God, I AM ANEW from A to F. Meditate on these transformations.

God, in You, I AM ANEW from the broken feature of . . .	With the beautiful feature of . . .
A – Anger	A – Acceptance
B – Betrayal	B – Benevolence
C – Criticism	C – Compassion
D – Distracted	D – Disciplined
E – Envy	E – Empathy
F – Fearful	F – Forgiveness

🩶🤍 CHAPTER 8 – G FEATURES
Grief to Grateful

Dear God, thank You that I am transformed and made ANEW from the broken feature of GRIEF with the beautiful feature of GRATEFUL by You.

Grief is a normal part of life. It means I've allowed myself to love and care about others. Life is full of painful losses. I have lost a parent and a child to death, a spouse and a house through divorce, jobs, boyfriends, friends, pets, struggled with infertility, health challenges, and had other losses. The hurt has faded over time when I have been grateful for what I was given while I had it. I get to, rather than have to accept the gifts I had, no matter how short-lived they were.

After my son died, I was devastated. It felt like an anvil was on my heart for more than a year and each breath was a struggle to take. I cried every day for a year, but God's hands are big enough to hold each tear I needed to cry. God sent me a wonderful friend to drag me out of bed for the first five months after his death, God has not stopped healing my heart.

Love doesn't die when our loved ones pass on to the next life; death cannot quench love. I still grow with love for my son and treasure the joys he brought and still brings me. I was able to see his bright eyes, hear him cry, rock him to sleep, and even hold him as I said goodbye when he took his last breath. It was also his life, not his death, that brought his twin brothers into the world after years of infertility. I count these as blessings knowing that many families affected by natural and human disasters never get to say goodbye and many mothers never get to hear their child cry before their child is returned to heaven.

Even still, it is a challenge to be grateful when grieving. *"There is a time for everything, and a season for every activity under the heavens: . . . a time to weep and a time to laugh, a time to mourn and a time to dance. . ." (Ecclesiastes 3:1, 4-5).* On the other side of tragedy is a triumph. God does for me what I cannot do for myself. He carries me through those dark places, turning my heartache into laughter and dancing.

Something to Think About

Each loss in life can open our hearts to love deeper if we let it. The Lord is on the other side of trauma and pain. *We need "not grieve like the rest of mankind, who have no hope" (1 Thessalonians 4:13).* Life is a series of mountains and valleys, of laughter and tears. I believe tears are rain to the soul.

Today I get to focus on laughter and the view from the mountain tops of life. The only way to avoid loss and grief is to avoid love. Yet, that is not how I want to live. Living without love is meaningless to me. Be willing to risk loss by choosing to risk love. Remember that pain, loss, and grief are inevitable, but continual suffering is optional.

Life is lighter when I fill it with grateful memories and lessons learned. Maybe the very things that cause grief can be a source of gratitude that can lead to rebirth and renewed faith in Christ.

Quote to Ponder

"Your joy is your sorrow unmasked. . . The deeper that sorrow carves into your being, the more joy you can contain. . . When you are sorrowful look again in your heart, and you shall see that in truth you are weeping for that which has been your delight" (Gibran 29).

Take Action

Write, draw, pray, meditate, and reflect in ANEW's companion journal as follows:

Broken Feature:	Beautiful Feature:
Dear God, thank You for transforming the broken feature of GRIEF into something beautiful.	Dear God, thank You for transforming the beautiful feature of GRATEFUL into something even more beautiful.

Questions beyond the introductory suggestions

- Have I allowed myself to feel the sadness and to grieve the deaths and losses in my life?
- Do I know it's okay to both miss and love my loved ones who've passed away, even years or decades later?
- Can I make a gratitude list of the blessings that I received from the people and things that I've lost?
- How have I opened my heart to deeper levels of love because of the losses I've experienced?

♥♥ CHAPTER 9 – H FEATURES
Helpless to Hopeful

Dear God, thank You that I am transformed and made ANEW from the broken feature of HELPLESS with the beautiful feature of HOPEFUL by You.

Admitting my powerlessness over situations that are outside of my control does not mean helpless. Instead, I get to turn to Jesus and invite His power into my life. I have hope that I can experience relief from pain and receive healing. By letting go, I allow the Lord to take over control of the person, place, thing, or situation that is causing me pain or stress.

Somewhere along the way, I learned that I had to take care of the people in my life in the hopes that they would reciprocate and care for me. This strategy rarely resulted in getting my needs met. Over the years, I've learned to put my trust in Jesus to care for my loved ones and me.

God is the director, and I am but one actor in the play of life. I am not in control. He can work through me and through others to bring about His will and plan for each of our lives. Things work out best when I get out of God's way, and just do the next indicated action in my life. I take care of myself by letting God be in charge.

How can I take care of myself? I do so by setting priorities, making time for prayer, meditating on the scriptures, and connecting with the Holy Spirit. I get to balance the different aspects of my life instead of getting overextended to my detriment. Today, I also make time for sleep, exercise, fun, work, healthy eating, setting goals, and maintaining healthy boundaries with others.

Something to Think About

Miracles happen when I take my hands off the wheel of life and put my faith in the Lord. It may seem like a paradox, yet if I admit and accept my powerlessness that's when I gain hope and power from the Holy Spirit to change my life.

When my hope is rooted in Jesus Christ, I no longer feel helpless. I get to release my illusion of control and let God do for me what I cannot do for myself.

If I do the footwork in my faith journey each day, the Lord takes care of me. By focusing on my relationship with Him first, the rest of the world seems to fall into place.

Quote to Ponder

"May the God of hope fill you with all joy and peace as you trust in him, so that you may overflow with hope by the power of the Holy Spirit" (Romans 15:13).

Take Action

Write, draw, pray, meditate, and reflect in ANEW's companion journal as follows:

Broken Feature:	Beautiful Feature:
Dear God, thank You for transforming the broken feature of HELPLESS into something beautiful.	Dear God, thank You for transforming the beautiful feature of HOPEFUL into something even more beautiful.

Questions beyond the introductory suggestions

- Do I realize that my hope comes from accepting my powerlessness and tapping into the power of God in Christ?
- When did I first feel helpless as a child? As an adult? Today?
- In what instances did I put my hope in God and my prayers were answered?
- How can I pray to let God be in charge instead of me?

❤ ♡ CHAPTER 10 – I FEATURES
Isolation to Intimacy

Dear God, thank You that I am transformed and made ANEW from the broken feature of ISOLATION with the beautiful feature of INTIMACY by You.

Jesus is the greatest example of being intimate with the Father, himself, and others. Each day, he made time connecting with God a top priority. He also took care of his needs by sleeping, walking, eating, laughing, and working. He then reached out with an open heart to hear, feel, and share God's love. Yet, when he was tired or overwhelmed, instead of pushing himself, he would leave the crowds to rest and pray to get filled up again.

When I get preoccupied or burdened with my life and my struggles, I hide from God and others. Yet, that is when I need them the most. Taking care of myself starts with prioritizing time with the Lord for scripture reading, prayer, and meditation each day. My relationship with myself deepens as I receive His unconditional acceptance, forgiveness, and love.

In this way, I am filled up spiritually and emotionally by the Holy Spirit, and I am prompted to shower myself with self-love. This means I treat myself the way I would treat a best friend. I take care of my needs for sleep, exercise, healthy eating, work, play, and rest. The result is my cup runs over with abundance.

I break free of isolation by filling myself up with the love and power of Jesus Christ and with self-care. Then, I reach out and risk intimacy with others with a heart overflowing with love from the Father. As I've taken care of myself, I can freely give to others genuinely without strings attached. Sometimes, I provide a supportive shoulder to cry on or a hug to let others know they are loved just the way they are. As a result, I receive friendship and intimacy from others.

Something to Think About

Isolation is a lonely place. When I withdraw from life and other people for too long, I cut myself off from love and intimacy. Even in a crowd, I can still feel separated from others by not disclosing my authentic self. This is when I need to connect with God, knowing He loves me unconditionally.

"In your relationships with one another, have the same mindset as Christ Jesus" (Philippians 2:5). Jesus accepted and reached out to people with intimacy. I can do the same by caring for my family and friends and letting them love me back.

Intimacy is risky. Intimate relationships break me out of isolation. I may get hurt by opening my heart to others, but it's worth the risk. When I take part in life and receive God's love and share it with others, I grow and transform. In this way, I create healthy relationships.

Quote to Ponder

"Does it occur to God that it is hard for us to live with only His invisible presence; that sometimes we long for human arms to give us a hug?" (Roper 1994, pp. 138-40).

Take Action

Write, draw, pray, meditate, and reflect in ANEW's companion journal as follows:

Broken Feature:	Beautiful Feature:
Dear God, thank You for transforming the broken feature of ISOLATION into something beautiful.	Dear God, thank You for transforming the beautiful feature of INTIMACY into something even more beautiful.

Questions beyond the introductory suggestions

- Who can I say hello and offer a smile today?
- How can I reach out to a close family member or friend today with a call or a visit to share a laugh or get a hug?
- Where can I join a church small group, self-help meeting, volunteer organization, online group, or fun meetup to get closer to others this week?
- What one person can I open my heart to deeper levels of love and intimacy this month?

🖤🤍 CHAPTER 11 – J FEATURES
Judgment to Joyful

Dear God, thank You that I am transformed and made ANEW from the broken feature of JUDGMENT with the beautiful feature of JOYFUL by You.

Judgments are necessary at a court of law but far less valuable in relationships. In our plastic society, we try to look happy and perfect on the outside. I assume this is how other people feel on the inside. Yet the truth is we're human, we have bad days, and we screw up.

The learning process includes making mistakes to learn from them and make more. Practice makes for more practice, not perfection. No one escapes the microscope we put ourselves and others under. When I judge myself and others, Jesus says I put myself in the role of God. I am not God.

The joy of the Lord is a byproduct of inner gratitude and peace. It produces happiness in the world around me. It results from giving my observations and opinions to the Lord as well as accepting His forgiveness when I have erred. He is a merciful and gracious judge of me and others.

I want to be happy, joyous, and free. I can do that by leaving judgments to God. Jesus said, *"Do not judge, or you too will be judged. . . Why do you look at the speck of sawdust in your brother's eye and pay no attention to the plank in your own eye?" (Matthew 7:1, 3).* Today, I refuse to let anyone or anything rob me of joy by leading me away from God's prompting to look at refining my brokenness and letting Him transform me.

Do I want to be happy, or do I want to be right? It's usually one or the other, not both. When I let the Lord be in charge, the peace inside me results in joy around me. As I receive His love and forgiveness, I offer the same to myself and others. I can trust that we do the best we can and leave the rest to Him.

Something to Think About

I don't have all the answers, but the Lord does. When I point my finger at someone, I have three fingers pointing back at me. I've heard it said, "If you spot it, you've got it." So, let me focus on working out my salvation instead of acting like God.

I get to put down the magnifying glass and pick up the mirror, allowing myself and others to be human. God reminds me that we each do our best with the information, emotions, and tools we have at any given moment. Remembering that we all are under different pressures helps me give myself and others a break.

Judgment, criticism, sarcasm, gossip, snide remarks, and eye-rolling have no place in my life or my relationships. I can look for the good in others and keep my life peaceful. I desire a life filled with joy that overflows into happiness from me to others.

Quote to Ponder

"As the Father has loved me, so have I loved you. Now remain in my love. . . I have told you this so that my joy may be in you and that your joy may be complete. My command is this: Love each other as I have loved you." (John 15:9, 11-12).

Take Action

Write, draw, pray, meditate, and reflect in ANEW's companion journal as follows:

Broken Feature:	Beautiful Feature:
Dear God, thank You for transforming the broken feature of JUDGMENT into something beautiful.	Dear God, thank You for transforming the beautiful feature of JOYFUL into something even more beautiful.

Questions beyond the introductory suggestions

- When did I smile the most and feel the happiest when I was a kid? What was I doing? Who was I with?
- Am I willing to give myself and others a break, knowing that as humans we are meant to practice and make mistakes to learn?
- What mistakes do I keep judging in others? Am I willing to look at myself for those same errors?
- When will I make time for that person, comedian, or show that makes me belly laugh?

❤ ♥ CHAPTER 12 – K FEATURES
Killjoy to Kindness

Dear God, thank You that I am transformed and made ANEW from the broken feature of KILLJOY with the beautiful feature of KINDNESS by You.

Hurry is the enemy of kindness. When I'm in a hurry, I speak too quickly instead of listening carefully. This can hurt the people I love. Jesus was never in a hurry and he always listened intently. He made time to be there for people. He felt people's hurts before he healed them.

I realize that many times I have unconsciously been unfeeling and a killjoy when I made suggestions instead of just listening and caring. Most of the time, it is nicer to withhold my opinions than to make observations. Advice, especially unsolicited, is unkind. If I feel an urge to say something, I could say, "I know you can figure this out" or "I'll be here each step of the way."

I may want to consider that I don't have the foggiest idea of the exact nature of what my loved one is going through. I might consider giving other people the benefit of the doubt that they are doing the best they can with their situation. I could offer a supportive word. Then I can pray that my loved one will be given direction and guidance by the Lord.

My grandmother was the most gracious person I ever knew. Each time she would see me, she'd sing, "Good, good, good, and nice, nice, nice, and kind, kind, kind, that's you, that's you!" After hearing it enough times from someone who loved me, I began to believe it for myself. It is a song that I used to sing to my kids when they were little.

Something to Think About

Jesus shared the parable of the Good Samaritan in the gospel of Luke. Both the priest and the Levite were too busy to stop and help the badly, beaten man in the road. Yet, the Samaritan was kind as he stopped and took time to bandage and nurse the man back to health even through the night.

When my focus is on helping and listening to other people, I am loving people like God loves the world. It's not my job to point out other people's shortcomings. I want to be the friend who elevates others instead of tearing them down.

One of the nicest things I can say is, "I believe in you!" or "I will pray for you!" One of the most loving things I can do is cheer for someone's dreams. I can offer a listening ear, a warm hug, and words of love and encouragement for the people in my life. I know that when I am gentle with myself and others, life goes more smoothly.

Quote to Ponder

"But the fruit of the Spirit is love, joy, peace, patience, kindness, goodness, faithfulness, gentleness and self-control" (Galatians 5:22-3).

Take Action

Write, draw, pray, meditate, and reflect in ANEW's companion journal as follows:

Broken Feature:	Beautiful Feature:
Dear God, thank You for transforming the broken feature of KILLJOY into something beautiful.	Dear God, thank You for transforming the beautiful feature of KINDNESS into something even more beautiful.

Questions beyond the introductory suggestions

- Who was the kindest person in my childhood? How about today?
- What is the nicest thing that anyone has said to me?
- How did I feel when I shared something with a friend and instead of a supportive ear, I got a bunch of advice?
- In what areas of my life do I need to slow down, so I can eliminate hurry?

💕 CHAPTER 13 – L FEATURES
Lonely to Loved

Dear God, thank You that I am transformed and made ANEW from the broken feature of LONELY with the beautiful feature of LOVED by You.

It was very lonely while growing up in a divorced and alcoholic family. I was embarrassed to bring kids to my mom's house as she was often drunk. At my dad's place, I only had time to study with fellow students. As a result, I had very few friends, which meant I had almost no one in whom to confide.

Everything was a secret, so I rarely, if ever, felt comfortable sharing what was on my mind with my parents or extended family. I felt scared and alone most of the time. Then I found Alateen and I learned about the unconditional love of God. I no longer felt alone. I made friends with kids, who understood what it was like living with an alcoholic parent.

While working on the Twelve Steps of Alateen, which is part of Al-Anon, I learned about a loving Higher Power and came to believe in Jesus Christ. I believe as the apostle John shared, *"God is love" (1 John 4:8).* He already cared for me before I even knew Him and before I could love myself or anyone else.

The Lord already knows all my secrets and accepts me anyway. *"For God so loved the world that he gave his one and only Son, that whoever believes in him shall not perish but have eternal life" (John 3:16).* The Father cares so much for the world that he sent Jesus to live an example of the most beautiful life, sacrifice himself for us, and forgive our brokenness. This love flows from Him to me and from me to others.

Something to Think About

Trust is the foundation of love. The Father has graciously shown us His love by sending His son, Jesus Christ. When I receive His love, I can more easily give it to myself and others.

I trust that the Lord is already running towards me with open arms. He already cares for me, even when I don't feel that I deserve it. God opens doors for me to love and be loved by others.

Even still, with the nearly unlimited opportunities to connect with others using technology, for many, the world still feels like a lonely place. As technology advances, we often stay online more and away from people.

Love takes time and effort to grow. To feel connected, I take the risk and reach out to others with God's love in my heart. Small face-to-face church groups, self-help meetings, classes, and fun meetups are places where I make real friends. When I accept love how people offer it without condition, I no longer feel alone.

Quote to Ponder

"'Teacher, which is the greatest commandment in the Law?' Jesus replied: 'Love the Lord your God with all your heart and with all your soul and with all your mind.' This is the first and greatest commandment. And the second is like it: Love your neighbor as yourself'" (Matthew 22:36-9).

Take Action

Write, draw, pray, meditate, and reflect in ANEW's companion journal as follows:

Broken Feature:	Beautiful Feature:
Dear God, thank You for transforming the broken feature of LONELY into something beautiful.	Dear God, thank You for transforming the beautiful feature of LOVED into something even more beautiful.

Questions beyond the introductory suggestions

- Have I accepted the amazing love of God by asking Jesus Christ into my heart and life to be my Lord and Savior, knowing that he would have died for me alone?
- Am I ready to love myself the way God already loves me?
- What am I doing that is keeping me lonely and away from people who will love me just the way I am?
- Who are the people and where are the places I go to that feel the most loving to me, such as a church, family, friends, self-help meetings, or meetup groups?

💗💗 CHAPTER 14 – REFLECTIONS
Features from G to L

Dear God, thank You that I am transformed and made ANEW from these G to L broken features with beautiful ones by You.

God is making me ANEW from G to L! Use this day to catch up, rest, and/or reflect on these questions in ANEW's companion journal:

- What have I done this week that has reduced grief and brought me joy and happiness? How can I do more of it?
- Who are the people and where are the places I've identified that show me love and kindness?
- How can I break out of isolation, drop judgments, and develop intimate connections to help me overcome the pain of these broken features from G to L?

Quote to Ponder

"Love is patient, love is kind. It does not envy, it does not boast, it is not proud. It does not dishonor others, it is not self-seeking, it is not easily angered, it keeps no record of wrongs. Love does not delight in evil but rejoices with the truth. It always protects, always trusts, always hopes, always perseveres. Love never fails" (1 Corinthians 13:4-8).

With God, I AM ANEW from G to L. Meditate on these transformations.

God, in You, I AM ANEW from the broken feature of . . .	With the beautiful feature of . . .
G – Grief	G – Grateful
H – Helpless	H – Hopeful
I – Isolation	I – Intimacy
J – Judgment	J – Joyful
K – Killjoy	K – Kindness
L – Lonely	L – Loved

💙 🤍 CHAPTER 15 – M FEATURES
Misfit to Masterpiece

Dear God, thank You that I am transformed and made ANEW from the broken feature of MISFIT with the beautiful feature of MASTERPIECE by You.

Sometimes I feel insignificant. That's when I remember that the mighty oak tree lives in the tiny acorn. It is natural to feel less than when I stumble. Yet, I am not a mistake because I make mistakes. My value comes from God working within me, not the total of the blunders I've made in the past.

The various pieces of my life fit together to create a masterful tapestry. The front of such a weaving looks beautiful and intricate. It is the part of my life that God sees the radiance in me. Yet, I live on the backside of it most of the time. That is where the tangled strings and knots are visible. I look at the areas of struggle, growth, sadness, loss, and pain in my life from the backside, and I feel like a hot mess. Yet, the Lord can take the challenges of my life and turn them into masterpieces.

Slowly, as I grow in my spiritual journey, I consider a God-like perspective of my life. Then I suddenly realize these areas of struggle are often the most transformational parts of my life. This shift reminds me of His master plan for me.

By following Jesus first, I recognized my powerlessness and accepted God's power to transform my broken features into beautiful ones. The features of my life that I considered broken often took root as survival instincts in my family of origin and are still present in my adult life from time to time. He taught me to look at my past in a redemptive light. Soon, I began to allow the power of love to make me a masterpiece.

Something to Think About

Do the people I love make mistakes? Yes, and I do, too. Let me first seek to forgive myself and others for not measuring up to my biased and often impossible standards. Thank God that our mistakes are part of the masterpieces of each of our lives.

The winds of the Holy Spirit help me soar. I have the power to let go of my past and become anew. I desire to see myself through God's loving and forgiving eyes. He masterfully transforms me daily from feeling like a misfit into the masterpiece I already am. I help Him do this by accepting both the brokenness and beauty in me each day.

Instead of focusing on how stuck I often feel, I look at how the Lord is weaving the struggles I have overcome in my past into the colorful tapestry of my life. I stand amazed at how He restores me each day. I am God's masterpiece.

Quote to Ponder

"For we are God's workmanship, created in Christ Jesus to do good works, which God prepared in advance for us to do" *(Ephesians 2:10).*

Take Action

Write, draw, pray, meditate, and reflect in ANEW's companion journal as follows:

Broken Feature:	Beautiful Feature:
Dear God, thank You for transforming the broken feature of MISFIT into something beautiful.	Dear God, thank You for transforming the beautiful feature of MASTERPIECE into something even more beautiful.

Questions beyond the introductory suggestions

- Am I willing to see that I am supposed to make mistakes to learn from them instead of being a misfit?
- Who are the people in my life who see my past struggles in God's redeeming light?
- Where can I go to feel loved as I am not just despite my mistakes, but for gaining victory over them?
- How can I see the tiny acorn that God has planted in my life to grow me into a mighty oak tree?

💙 CHAPTER 16 – N FEATURES
Nervous to Nurturing

Dear God, thank You that I am transformed and made ANEW from the broken feature of NERVOUS with the beautiful feature of NURTURING by You.

It is so easy to feel nervous when I'm trying to take care of the problems of other people and outside situations. Anxiety can consume me as dozens of catastrophic scenarios and outcomes run through my mind for myself, my loved ones, and even the world. I soon am no longer living in the present or allowing God to have a hand in my life. The Lord wants me to call on Him, but I was blocking his peace and power from entering my life by getting uptight and stressed out.

To stop the worry train, I remember to pause. I first start by exhaling slowly and then take a minute or so to take deep belly breaths. I often realize that I've been holding my breath for a long time. Once my body is calmed by my relaxed breathing, I pray to claim the promises in the scriptures. This allows God's breath of life to nurture my body and His word to calm my mind and soul.

When I feel anxiety, worry, or nervousness, I choose to focus on this day only. I can do this by pausing, praying, and asking God to release my anxieties. He then reminds me that He is bigger than my problems and His solutions are beyond what I can fathom. This helps me to let go of my often, misdirected solutions and depend on the solutions that the Lord has set in motion. I can remember that most challenges are God-sized ones.

Something to Think About

When I get out of God's way, He can take over. I choose to trust that He can use my life's brokenness to achieve the goals and solve the trials ahead of me. The best way for me to care for myself and others is to pray for blessings on our future and to live in today.

When I focus on growing the nurturing skills in my life, I can more freely offer a gentle heart, a loving hug, and a listening ear to others. Sometimes a simple phrase like "you can do it," or "I know you'll figure it out," is the most encouraging thing I can say to myself and others.

Let me be a wellspring of love that nurtures my family members, my friends, and me. When I spend my time accepting life on life's terms and looking for the best in myself and others, I more easily create positive relationships.

Quote to Ponder

"Therefore I tell you, do not worry about your life, what you will eat or drink; or about your body, what you will wear. Is not life more important than food, and the body more than clothes? Look at the birds of the air; they do not sow or reap or store away in barns, and yet your heavenly Father feeds them. Are you not much more valuable than they?" (Matthew 6:25-6).

Take Action

Write, draw, pray, meditate, and reflect in ANEW's companion journal as follows:

Broken Feature:	Beautiful Feature:
Dear God, thank You for transforming the broken feature of NERVOUS into something beautiful.	Dear God, thank You for transforming the beautiful feature of NURTURING into something even more beautiful.

Questions beyond the introductory suggestions

- When do I feel most nervous during the day?
- What activities nurture my mind, body, and spirit?
- How can I pray to let go and ask God to be in charge of my anxious heart?
- Who can I spend time with today, who nurtures me and calms my fears?

♥ ♥ CHAPTER 17 – O FEATURES
Opinionated to Open-Minded

Dear God, thank You that I am transformed and made ANEW from the broken feature of OPINIONATED with the beautiful feature of OPEN-MINDED by You.

As a strong-willed child, I was very opinionated. I believed I had the answers to life's questions, and other people needed to hear them. I couldn't have been more wrong. Then God opened my eyes and ears.

At my self-help and small group meetings, I heard, "You could be right." I found this phrase to be helpful when I was open-minded enough to accept that someone else's information, assessment, or opinion might be right. I realized sometimes I was right, and other times I was wrong.

I have opinions, which is good. That's not the issue. The crux of the matter is whether I feel compelled to share them, refuse to see anyone else's point of view, or blind myself to other possibilities. I choose to be open-minded to what people say to me, or I might miss solutions that God may show me through them. Several times in scripture, Jesus opened the eyes of the blind literally and figuratively.

Do I think my way is the right way? Maybe I'm clinging too tightly to my opinion of myself or too loosely to my faith in the Lord. When I am open to the Holy Spirit's guidance for my life and my loved ones' lives, I start to see how He is working things out and often in ways beyond my imagination. I remember to stay open to the seemingly circuitous path where I am being led. I want to walk the journey of life with Jesus.

Something to Think About

Am I so obstinate and closed-minded that I do not think what other people have to say is worth considering? Do I usually respond to comments and questions with the word "but"? If so, maybe I can open myself up to new ideas.

There are often many solutions to the same challenge. For instance, if I wanted a swimming pool in my backyard, there are many ways to go about it. I could buy an above ground pool and install it myself. Another way might be to rent a backhoe and hire a contractor to dig and install an inground pool. Lastly, I could even buy a new house that already has one.

When I'm open-minded, I stop playing God and let other people find solutions to their challenges. He alone knows the best path for them, not me, so I get to let go and give people grace to find the way He is leading them. Also, I receive His grace and patience when I am waiting on Him to direct my steps for the struggles in my life.

Quote to Ponder

"Then will the eyes of the blind be opened and the ears of the deaf unstopped" (Isaiah 35:5).

Take Action

Write, draw, pray, meditate, and reflect in ANEW's companion journal as follows:

Broken Feature:	Beautiful Feature:
Dear God, thank You for transforming the broken feature of OPINIONATED into something beautiful.	Dear God, thank You for transforming the beautiful feature of OPEN-MINDED into something even more beautiful.

Questions beyond the introductory suggestions

- Were my thoughts, feelings, and opinions valued as a child? If not, could that be why I'm opinionated instead of open-minded?
- Am I willing to admit that I can be wrong and other people could be right?
- Do I push my opinions on people without listening to their point of view?
- How can I pause and open my mind to what my loved ones have to say without saying "but" to interject my thoughts?

❤ ❀ CHAPTER 18 – P FEATURES
Perfectionism to Prayerful

Dear God, thank You that I am transformed and made ANEW from the broken feature of PERFECTIONISM with the beautiful feature of PRAYERFUL by You.

"The Serenity Prayer" is a well-known poem that holds much wisdom. It begins as follows, "God, grant me the serenity to accept the things I cannot change; courage to change the things I can; and wisdom to know the difference. Living one day at a time; enjoying one moment at a time; accepting hardships as the pathway to peace" (Niebuhr 1934). In Christian and self-help communities, I get to change the things that are in my control, live in this moment only, and leave the rest to God. This includes other people and my past mistakes. I also get to change myself, particularly my attitudes and my actions.

A perfect human being is an oxymoron. No one is perfect, including me. Being a perfectly, imperfect human is what the Lord desires. We make mistakes until we learn their lessons, and then we get to make more of them and repeat the cycle. If I miss the mark, I need not miss the lessons that God teaches me. It is not productive to beat myself up for yesterday's decisions with today's information.

Prayer is an intimate time with the Lord when I ask for His advice and meditate by listening to His response. It frees me of life's burdens and invites His blessings into my life. *"The prayer of a righteous person is powerful and effective"*

(James 5:16). Prayer helps me let go of my illusion of control and detach from people, places, and things. Then I can more easily ask for God's power to transform me.

Something to Think About

Each day I get to take off my junior God button and seek the Lord. When I get up in the morning and get down on my knees in prayer, things just seem to fall into place. If I get out of His way and let Him do for me what I cannot do for myself, miracles happen.

When I start my day humble before the Lord, things just seem to go better. I feel the power of the Holy Spirit working in my life to do the work of transformation, and it starts with a prayer. One of my favorite prayers came from my youngest son, which is "Thank you God for You God."

We are called *to* *"Rejoice always, pray continually, give thanks in all circumstances; for this is God's will for you in Christ Jesus"* *(1 Thessalonians 15:16-18).* The Holy Spirit directs me when I read my Bible, pray, and meditate on the love of God in Christ. Praying throughout the day brings peace and serenity, remembering I am not in control, but Jesus is.

Quote to Ponder

"Prayer is about God's grace, not us. Prayer is not about asking, but about aligning our spirits with God's spirit, our wills with God's will, and our ways with God's way" (Weaver 51).

Take Action

Write, draw, pray, meditate, and reflect in ANEW's companion journal as follows:

Broken Feature:	Beautiful Feature:
Dear God, thank You for transforming the broken feature of PERFECTION-ISM into something beautiful.	Dear God, thank You for transforming the beautiful feature of PRAYERFUL into something even more beautiful.

Questions beyond the introductory suggestions

- Did I have to prove that I was good enough, be constantly on the honor roll in school, or perform perfectly to feel loved and accepted in my youth?
- Have people in my life compared and shamed me when I did not do things perfectly?
- Am I willing to offer prayers of forgiveness, acceptance, and love for myself and others as perfectly, imperfect human beings who are supposed to make mistakes?
- Am I willing to take off my junior God button, and trust God with my humble prayers?

♥ ♪ CHAPTER 19 – Q FEATURES
Quarrelsome to Quiet

Dear God, thank You that I am transformed and made ANEW from the broken feature of QUARRELSOME with the beautiful feature of QUIET by You.

It was very noisy in my home when I was growing up with an alcoholic parent. There were lots of heated arguments and sometimes shouting. We each had something important to say and felt that it was necessary to share it or more often shove it down my throat. I received a long laundry list of the things I had to do to fix my life, even from people whose lives were totally out of control.

It is normal to have differences in understanding and to argue about conflicting thoughts some of the time. We want to feel heard by our loved one. Yet, that does not mean raising my voice over the voices of others to get them to listen to me.

If I say something once, my words are informative. When I repeat myself two, three, or many times, I've become controlling. The Bible explains how to live a peaceful life, *"Everyone should be quick to listen, slow to speak and slow to become angry, because human anger does not produce the righteousness that God desires" (James 1:19-20).* I need not argue. Even when I want to respond quickly, I am learning to be quiet and reflective.

Sometimes the kindest thing I can say is nothing. Now that I have a family of my own, I am learning to say less. My children have strong wills and want to share them with me. I ask God to hold my tongue so I can let them share and feel heard.

Something to Think About

If I have gotten into a fight with two or more people today, maybe I'm the one who ought to change my attitude. Sometimes I'm arguing just to hear myself speak instead of listening to what God and others want to share with me.

When I find it difficult to be silent, I realize that peace and serenity are absent from my life. Have I been going a hundred miles an hour in a million different directions? Likely yes. Have I taken time to meditate, pray, or spend time with God today? Probably no. When I'm in this place of chaos, I get to pause and be still, so I can listen to the whisper of the Lord.

It can be difficult for me to wait for the Lord's will and plan to show up in my life and the lives of others. Forcing solutions and opinions on others keeps me stirred up. If I can quiet my mind, body, and spirit, I can receive peace and serenity from the Holy Spirit. Daily, I get to turn away from the chaos around me and turn towards a quiet place where I can experience His will for my life.

Quote to Ponder

"Be still, and know that I am God; I will be exalted among the nations, I will be exalted in the earth" (Psalm 46:10).

Take Action

Write, draw, pray, meditate, and reflect in ANEW's companion journal as follows:

Broken Feature:	Beautiful Feature:
Dear God, thank You for transforming the broken feature of QUARRELSOME into something beautiful.	Dear God, thank You for transforming the beautiful feature of QUIET into something more beautiful.

Questions beyond the introductory suggestions

- Was my childhood noisy with quarreling or did my parents take time for silence? How about my home now?
- Where can I go and what can I do to quiet my mind and body so I can connect with the Holy Spirit?
- Can I accept that sometimes the best thing to say or do is nothing?
- Am I willing to turn away from the chaos of the world and be still with the Lord for at least one minute each day? How about ten minutes or more?

CHAPTER 20 – R FEATURES
Regret to Reverent

Dear God, thank You that I am transformed and made ANEW from the broken feature of REGRET with the beautiful feature of REVERENT by You.

I've made mistakes in the past, and I expect to make more each day. I rarely experience success if I haven't risked failure. When I look back on my life, I can do so with either regret for not being perfect or with reverence for being a work in progress.

Asking God for guidance on ways I can forgive humbles me to release the grip of unresolved guilt. I get to make amends when I've done or said something wrong or hurtful. I choose to create harmony in my life by honoring myself and others for our weaknesses and mistakes, rather than building up resentments and anger.

Sometimes my regrets are not over what I did that hurt someone else, but what I didn't do or didn't say that injured them. I also lament not following my dreams. Yet, when I make amends to myself and others, I get to regain the courage and faith to live out those plans that the Holy Spirit has put in my heart. We receive forgiveness of sins when we accept Jesus Christ into our lives. We can let go of our mistakes and receive hope for a new future.

I mess up because I am human. Yet, I am still a beloved child of God. Knowing this, I get to be gentle with myself and others. I can be reverent and honor my mind, body, and spirit to break free of self-reproach. I no longer want to look back wondering what I could have done.

Something to Think About

The fastest way to be offended is to take offense. When someone has wronged me, I remember the call to *"submit to one another out of reverence for Christ" (Ephesians 5:21).* It does not matter how recent or how long ago the offense occurred, whether accidentally or purposefully. The choice is mine to forgive and show reverence as well as gentleness to others for our humanity.

I release the grip of my past errors when I make amends to others and myself. At any time, I can choose to change and simultaneously let go of regrets and self-condemnation. They are rooted in vanity as I put myself above the Lord. Additionally, when I hold back forgiveness, I hurt myself.

Going forward, I get to focus on what I did with faith and God's plans for me. Free from the weight of unresolved mistakes from my past, the future is mine for the taking.

Quote to Ponder

"The very experiences that you have resented or regretted most in life—the ones you've wanted to hide and forget—are the experiences God wants to use to help others...You have to stop covering them up" (Warren 2012, p.247).

Take Action

Write, draw, pray, meditate, and reflect in ANEW's companion journal as follows:

Broken Feature:	Beautiful Feature:
Dear God, thank You for transforming the broken feature of REGRET into something beautiful.	Dear God, thank You for transforming the beautiful feature of REVERENT into something even more beautiful.

Questions beyond the introductory suggestions

- How can I let the Holy Spirit break the chains of unresolved guilt and past regrets?
- Have I asked God for forgiveness from past mistakes as His beloved child?
- Am I willing to be reverent to the Lord's will for my life and let Him be in charge of my future?
- Am I willing to honor others out of reverence for God?

CHAPTER 21 – REFLECTIONS
Features from M to R

Dear God, thank You that I am transformed and made ANEW from these M to R broken features with beautiful ones by You.

God is making me ANEW from M to R! Use this day to catch up, rest, and/or reflect on these questions in ANEW's companion journal:

- How can I set aside more time each day for quiet reflection on the scriptures and prayer in my life?
- Have I let go of regrets and accepted that God wants to take the mistakes, pain, hurt, and struggles of my past and turn them into a masterpiece?
- Am I willing to be reverent and open-minded about letting God transform the broken features from M to R into something beautiful?

Quote to Ponder

"Jesus replied, 'Truly I tell you, if you have faith and do not doubt, not only can you do what was done to the fig tree, but also you can say to this mountain, 'Go, throw yourself into the sea,' and it will be done. If you believe, you will receive whatever you ask for in prayer'" (Matthew 21:21-22).

With God, I AM ANEW from M to R. Meditate on these transformations.

God, in You, I AM ANEW from the broken feature of . . .	With the beautiful feature of . . .
M – Misfit	M - Masterpiece
N - Nervous	N - Nurturing
O - Opinionated	O - Open-Minded
P - Perfectionism	P - Prayerful
Q - Quarrelsome	Q - Quiet
R - Regret	R - Reverent

❤ 🤍 **CHAPTER 22 – S FEATURES**
Shame to Self-Esteem

Dear God, thank You that I am transformed and made ANEW from the broken feature of SHAME with the beautiful feature of SELF-ESTEEM by You.

In the dysfunctional family I grew up in, there wasn't much room for self-esteem. Instead, it was a breeding ground for shame. I couldn't fix my mom's alcoholism, although I thought I was the one responsible for doing just that. When her drinking progressed and she died now more than 20 years ago, I believed that I had failed. I didn't realize that she was sick. It took time to learn that I could never be enough to fix someone's addiction, only God is big enough for that. With His help, I let go of shame and forgave myself, knowing I did my best to help my mom.

As a Christian, I know *"there is now no condemnation for those who are in Christ Jesus" (Romans 8:1)*. God gave me a sense of guilt to prompt me to vulnerably share the wrongs I have done and to seek His forgiveness. In turn, I correct my behavior and make amends for harm I've caused. *"If we confess our sins, he is faithful and just and will forgive us our sins and purify us from all unrighteousness" (1 John 1:9)*.

Healthy guilt leads to reconciliation with God and grows my self-esteem. The Father loves His children enough to correct them. This is one important way that He lets me know that I am enough just as I am.

On the other hand, shame erodes my self-worth. It makes me feel that I am unworthy of love and redemption. It says I am not enough. Shame is a liar. The love of God in Christ triumphs over shame. *"As far as the east is from the west, so far has he removed our transgressions from us"* *(Psalm 103:12).*

Something to Think About

God is always bigger than shame. We are worthy of love and forgiveness because of His love in Jesus Christ. *"He is the atoning sacrifice for our sins, and not only for ours but also for the sins of the whole world" (1 John 2:2).*

I've learned that self-esteem reflects God's unconditional love and acceptance of me when I share my imperfect self with Him. By investigating the various aspects of my life, I can present my authentic self to the Lord for transformation.

When I accept, honor, forgive, and love each part of myself the way God already does, my self-esteem and feelings of worthiness can be built up. I soon feel that I am deserving of love and belonging to the family of the believers in the Lord.

As I let go of past mistakes, I see myself as more and more deserving of His love. I get to focus on how I'm growing myself day by day. Soon I begin to realize that I am enough for God.

Quote to Ponder

"We cultivate love when we allow our most vulnerable and powerful selves to be deeply seen and known...We can only love others as much as we love ourselves...Shame, blame, disrespect, betrayal, and the withholding of affection damage the roots from which love grows...True belonging is when we present our authentic, imperfect selves to the world. Our sense of belonging can never be greater than our level of self-acceptance" (Brown 2013, Session 1, starting at 28 minutes).

Take Action

Write, draw, pray, meditate, and reflect in ANEW's companion journal as follows:

Broken Feature:	Beautiful Feature:
Dear God, thank You for transforming the broken feature of SHAME into something beautiful.	Dear God, thank You for transforming the beautiful feature of SELF-ESTEEM into something even more beautiful.

Questions beyond the introductory suggestions

- In what areas of my life do I feel shame instead of forgiveness?
- Am I willing to accept that I am forgiven, worthy, and enough for God's love just as I am?
- When did I felt the proudest of myself? Can I list those times?
- What daily actions can I take to grow my self-esteem including making a habit of taking a personal inventory?

❤ ❥ CHAPTER 23 – T FEATURES
Thoughtless to Thoughtful

Dear God, thank You that I am transformed and made ANEW from the broken feature of THOUGHTLESS with the beautiful feature of THOUGHTFUL by You.

When I thoughtlessly speak or act, I hurt others. In my family of origin, there was little consideration before we spoke. I didn't care much about my words or my actions nor the damage they caused. That was until I accepted Jesus into my life and began my faith journey.

The Bible speaks a lot about controlling our words. *"With the tongue we praise our Lord and Father, and with it we curse human beings, who have been made in God's likeness. Out of the same mouth come praise and cursing. My brothers and sisters, this should not be" (James 3:9-10).*

When I pause before I say something, I have time to reflect on my thoughts. The acronym, THINK, is found at schools, churches, and support groups. It originated with the late pastor, Alan Redpath, of Moody Church in Chicago in the 1960s, who said, "THINK before you speak. Is it True, Helpful, Inspiring, Necessary, Kind?" (Habig 2008).

This acronym reminds me to take time to connect and seek God's will before I say or do anything. In this way, my response to a given situation is no longer a reaction but an act of love. When I ask the question above for the acronym, THINK, I keep myself from hurting others with my words.

This practice also teaches me to listen and respond with love, respect, and kindness.

Something to Think About

In the Bible, Paul encourages us to ponder what is beneficial. *"Finally, brothers and sisters, whatever is true, whatever is noble, whatever is right, whatever is pure, whatever is lovely, whatever is admirable—if anything is excellent or praiseworthy—think about such things" (Philippians 4:8).*

When I forget to pause before I speak, it gets me into trouble. It is normal to react and say something in haste. In those moments, I get to stop and THINK. Then I can forgive myself, make amends, and change my behavior.

Today, I get to pause and invite God into my heart so my words can be full of love and grace. As I become more present with my spirit, my thoughts and words become more like those of the Lord.

Quote to Ponder

"The choices you make determine the quality of the life you lead. Be thoughtful. Develop high standards and strict criteria for evaluating how you invest your time and energy. Base your choice not on what feels good in the moment but on what best serves your ultimate goals. Measure them according to your values and principles" (Vujicic 2013, p. 187).

Take Action

Write, draw, pray, meditate, and reflect in ANEW's companion journal as follows:

Broken Feature:	Beautiful Feature:
Dear God, thank You for transforming the broken feature of THOUGHTLESS into something beautiful.	Dear God, thank You for transforming the beautiful feature of THOUGHTFUL into something even more beautiful.

Questions beyond the introductory suggestions

- How do I feel when people interrupt me or respond without pausing before speaking?
- When have I spoken or acted thoughtlessly and it got me in trouble or hurt someone?
- Am I willing to pause to ask myself this question before I speak, "Is it true, helpful, inspiring, necessary, and kind?"
- Who in my life is thoughtful? How can I spend more time with those people?

❤️ CHAPTER 24 – U FEATURES
Uptight to Uplifting

Dear God, thank You that I am transformed and made ANEW from the broken feature of UPTIGHT with the beautiful feature of UPLIFTING by You.

It can be difficult for me to relax. Growing up in an alcoholic and dysfunctional family, I expected a new drama or tragedy to be right around the corner.

Home felt more like a rollercoaster ride, not knowing when the next turn or drop would happen. The unpredictability and chaos of this unsafe environment were both confusing and frightening.

I wanted to control and fix other people, especially my alcoholic mother. I was often anxious when I walked home from school, wondering if my mom would be drinking or in the hospital with another suicide attempt. I also took on her responsibilities, thinking I was uplifting, but I was just meddling in God's business.

Through self-help and church groups, the Lord has taught me about the power of prayer, which helps me to release my fears and encourage other people. The Lord can take away the uptight feelings in my life and release me of responsibility for my loved ones' lives.

Now that I have some experience with letting go and letting God, minding my own business is easier. He is in charge, not me. When I find myself slipping back into meddling behavior, the Lord reminds me to trust Him.

Something to Think About

As an adult, I still can assume the worst, which increases my anxiety. I tend to offer advice to others, thinking I'm being helpful, but often it is because I feel uptight and want to fix the outside world.

It is difficult for me to wait for solutions to unfold because I want to be in control. My interference is not supportive. It might be what is blocking God from teaching my loved ones the lessons that they ought to learn on their own.

If I already have an answer or a plan to help the moment my loved one opens his or her mouth, then I'm not at peace with God. To be uplifting, I listen patiently and then pray for the right words to share, if any. When I interrupt or respond too quickly, I hinder the Lord's influence on others and myself. He is in control, not me, even if I want to be in control.

A bird cannot fly if its wings are closed. When I'm feeling uptight, I feel like that bird. God wants me to open up my wings so I can soar. He has a plan for my life and for the challenges that I am facing. Let me let God and fly.

Quote to Ponder

"Do not let any unwholesome talk come out of your mouths, but only what is helpful for building others up according to their needs, that it may benefit those who listen." (Ephesians 4:29).

Take Action

Write, draw, pray, meditate, and reflect in ANEW's companion journal as follows:

Broken Feature:	Beautiful Feature:
Dear God, thank You for transforming the broken feature of UPTIGHT into something beautiful.	Dear God, thank You for transforming the beautiful feature of UPLIFTING into something even more beautiful.

Questions beyond the introductory suggestions

- How often have I assumed the worst and it never happened?
- When I feel uptight, am I willing to pause and pray for God to take away my fears?
- How can I mind my own business and focus on supporting my loved ones?
- Where can I go to be around people who encourage one another and are uplifting to me?

❤ ❤ CHAPTER 25 – V FEATURES
Victim to Victorious

Dear God, thank You that I am transformed and made ANEW from the broken feature of VICTIM with the beautiful feature of VICTORIOUS by You.

When I was growing up, I whined about how rough my life was. I complained about my parents' divorce, my mother's drinking, and the charade I put on to protect my mom. I considered myself a mere survivor of an alcoholic family.

Then I met other people who didn't have parents or who had been grossly abused by their caregivers. I realized they were not weighed down by the challenges in their lives; they overcame them. They accepted the past, forgave their parents or caregivers, and were living their lives in the present. I realized that they had victory over the hurts and abuses in their lives, while I was still a victim wallowing in self-pity.

Victory starts with my attitude, not my circumstances. Whether I win or lose, it is my attitude that makes me a winner. If I have a defeatist attitude, I cannot have victory. I get to believe that there is a brighter future. This hope is grounded in my relationship with God. He is the one who gives us victory in the Lord Jesus Christ. *"But thanks be to God! He gives us the victory through our Lord Jesus Christ"* *(1 Corinthians 15:57).*

When I believe that God is greater than my circumstances, I can overcome any challenge. He is always bigger! I gain victory over my life and my attitude by using the Serenity Prayer, as mentioned in Chapter 18. It starts with the word

"God." It reminds me and teaches me that He is in charge, not me (Niebuhr 1934).

Something to Think About

Is my attitude one of a victor or a victim? Today, I can overcome any challenge I face. When I realize the Lord is my life coach, I find victory over the trials of my life.

I remember that God isn't just at the finish line of the race, waiting to put an olive wreath on my head. He is also there at the start and during each step of the process from the beginning to the end. Jesus is my running mate in the game of life. This knowledge reassures me that the solutions are already a given, and to have hope in His plan.

In those circumstances that look like a defeat, God teaches me to use those setbacks as stepping-stones on my journey. I trust that He can work things out for the greater good, regardless of the outcome.

Quote to Ponder

"In all these things we are more than conquerors through [Christ] who loved us" (Romans 8:37).

Take Action

Write, draw, pray, meditate, and reflect in ANEW's companion journal as follows:

Broken Feature:	Beautiful Feature:
Dear God, thank You for transforming the broken feature of VICTIM into something beautiful.	Dear God, thank You for transforming the beautiful feature of VICTORIOUS into something even more beautiful.

Questions beyond the introductory suggestions

- What are the victories that are the most meaningful to me in my past?
- Am I willing to let go of the injuries and losses in my life, so I can shake off any sense of being a victim?
- Can I adopt the mindset of God, who sees and makes me into a conqueror each day?
- Who are the people in my life that see me as victorious?

♥ ♥ CHAPTER 26 – W FEATURES
Willful to Willing

Dear God, thank You that I am transformed and made ANEW from the broken feature of WILLFUL with the beautiful feature of WILLING by You.

It was with the least bit of willingness that I asked God for help from the chaos of my mom's alcoholism. It was with only a shred of readiness and a lot of resistance that my brother dragged me to my first self-help meeting called, Alateen, which is part of Al-Anon. The Twelve Steps led me to church and my faith in Jesus Christ as my Higher Power. I learned to accept my powerlessness and seek the Lord's guidance and wisdom.

King David gave this advice to the man who would become the wisest man in the world. *"And you, my son Solomon, acknowledge the God of your father, and serve him with wholehearted devotion and with a willing mind, for the Lord searches every heart and understands every motive behind the thoughts" (1 Chronicles 28:9).* We can heed this advice when we are willing enough to let God be God.

I have been a very strong-willed person since childhood, which is how I survived growing up with an alcoholic parent. There was a lot of fighting in my childhood home. I was stubborn, wanted to be right, and to win each discussion or argument. Yet, no one ever won, as it was a win-lose game.

There are places where competition is expected, like sports and contests. However, in my family and relationships, I've learned that it is better to compromise and to create win-win experiences. We can best do this when we accept each other, just as they are, and life exactly as it is.

Something to Think About

Today, I want to have peaceful relationships with family and friends. This means that everything isn't all about me or all about them. It's about us. We willingly listen to one another and keep the focus on love and kindness instead of self-centeredness.

If I close my ears and my mind, I am resisting growth and learning. When the same scenarios come up again and again in relationships, I realize God is telling me to surrender. His help is always available if I let Him in.

The insistence on being right to get my way keeps me from God's guidance. If I want to be happy, I willingly invite His Holy Spirit into my life.

Quote to Ponder

"To resist God is to resist our very truest selves. When we resist happiness we place a barrier between ourselves and God, a barrier between ourselves and the incredible people God created us to be, a barrier between ourselves and the wonderful life God dreamed for us" (Kelly 2016, p. 17).

Take Action

Write, draw, pray, meditate, and reflect in ANEW's companion journal as follows:

Broken Feature:	Beautiful Feature:
Dear God, thank You for transforming the broken feature of WILLFUL into something beautiful.	Dear God, thank You for transforming the beautiful feature of WILLING into something even more beautiful.

Questions beyond the introductory suggestions

- Was I a willful or a compliant child? How about now that I'm an adult?
- Am I willing to surrender my illusion of control so God can make miracles happen in my life?
- What scenarios keep coming up that could change if I stopped resisting the Holy Spirit's guidance?
- When have I willingly let God direct my steps? What happened?

♥ ♥ CHAPTER 27 – X FEATURES
eXtreme to eXpressive

Dear God, thank You that I am transformed and made ANEW from the broken feature of eXTREME with the beautiful feature of eXPRESSIVE by You.

While growing up, I lived a life of extremes. My mom struggled with manic depressive episodes. She was also a periodic alcoholic. I never knew if she would be happy to see me when I got home from school, at the psychiatric ward, or passed out drunk with the doors locked. It was so frightening that it felt like living in a war zone.

To cope, I took being in control of my thoughts and actions to the extreme. This helped me to survive the uncomfortable feelings in such an unpredictable and chaotic home. Over time, my life became black and white. I didn't know how to live in the grey. These extremes included words and silence, as well as actions and inactions.

At self-help meetings, I would explain at length the reasons for my horrible plight in life. Sometimes I went on and on about the many woes of my life, my mom's drinking and death, my parent's divorce, and my mom's boyfriend's abuses. I shared mainly about my sadness, anger, and hurt. I didn't know how to show restraint or express myself in relationships apart from extremes.

The Eleventh Step of Alateen brought me to the knowledge of the love of God in Christ. Now, I know I can cry out to the Lord in my distress. I've since learned after years in self-help and

Church groups to share more than just the experience of my story, by balancing it with my strength and hope.

Something to Think About

"I never speak in black and white" is a favorite saying that I heard at a Twelve Step meeting. My friends and I laugh at this saying now, and we remind each other when our conversations lose color and become extreme. However, in the early days of my faith journey and even today, when I feel a lot of pressure, I can still think that way.

Today I recognize that it is okay to express myself without dumping my life story and struggles on other people. It is okay for me to express joy and love without clouding it with past hurts, pain, or losses. It is equally acceptable to express sadness, anger, and frustration in healthy ways. I share my hurt feeling with safe people who can support me in my journey from unhappiness back to peace and serenity.

God gave us emotions so we could feel the full extent of our feelings: the joyful ones, the sad ones, the angry ones, the fearful ones, the victorious ones, and every feeling in between. I can best do that when I'm willing to paint my life in color, not just in black and white.

Quote to Ponder

"In my distress I called to the LORD; I cried to my God for help. From his temple he heard my voice; my cry came before him, into his ears." (Psalm 18:6).

Take Action

Write, draw, pray, meditate, and reflect in ANEW's companion journal as follows:

Broken Feature:	Beautiful Feature:
Dear God, thank You for transforming the broken feature of eXTREME into something beautiful.	Dear God, thank You for transforming the beautiful feature of eXPRESSIVE into something even more beautiful.

Questions beyond the introductory suggestions

- Do I think in black and white? Am I willing to accept that life has many more colors?
- How can I express my thoughts and feelings without becoming extreme?
- Where can I go to cry out to the Lord with the depth and breadth of my emotions?
- Who are safe people that I can express my deepest hurts and receive their experience, strength, and hope?

🖤🤍 CHAPTER 28 – REFLECTIONS
Features S to X

Dear God, thank You that I am transformed and made ANEW from these S to X broken features with beautiful ones by You.

God is making me ANEW from S to X! Use this day to catch up, rest, and/or reflect on these questions in ANEW's companion journal:

- Am I willing to let God remove the shame and victimization in my life so He can build my self-esteem?
- Will I let God be in charge so that He can lead me to victory?
- Which people in my life that are uplifting and expressive, and thoughtful? How can I spend more time with them?

Quote to Ponder

"Rejoice in the Lord always. I will say it again: Rejoice! Let your gentleness be evident to all. The Lord is near. Do not be anxious about anything, but in everything, by prayer and petition, with thanksgiving, present your requests to God" *(Philippians4:4-6).*

With God, I AM ANEW from S to X. Meditate on these transformations.

God, in You, I AM ANEW from the broken feature of . . .	With the beautiful feature of . . .
S – Shame	S - Self-Esteem
T – Thoughtless	T – Thoughtful
U – Uptight	U – Uplifting
V – Victim	V – Victorious
W – Willful	W – Willing
X – eXtreme	X – eXpressive

CHAPTER 29 – Y FEATURES
Yelling to Yielding

Dear God, thank You that I am transformed and made ANEW from the broken feature of YELLING with the beautiful feature of YIELDING by You.

In the alcoholic home of my childhood, yelling became commonplace while growing up. I remember how embarrassed I was to invite friends to my home after school or for dinner. It didn't feel normal, but I didn't know how to change it.

Being right felt more important than being happy. I didn't know how to defer to others' ideas or thoughts. By fighting with my family and others, I was shaking my fist at God.

Yielding, submission, and surrender felt weak until I allowed the power of God into my heart and life. In self-help communities, I learned there is but one authority, a loving Higher Power, which led me to faith in Jesus Christ.

At Al-Anon and church meetings, I was taught to yield to the group and others peacefully. Each person had time and space to complete their thought without interruption or feedback. This level of respect was a novel concept for me.

Eventually, my dad remarried, and my stepmom showed me how to yield and listen with an open heart instead of screaming to get my way. She even adopted me after my mom passed away.

Over time I've learned the only way to let God is to let go. Letting go of control leads to closer fellowship with loved ones and serenity in my spirit. When I surrender my life, my plan, and my will to the Lord Jesus Christ, I reap a harvest of love, hope, and blessings in my life.

Something to Think About

"Will this be important next year?" Asking this question is a great way to find contentment with what is. If what I am arguing about or insisting upon won't be significant in a year, then it might be worthwhile to drop my sword, raise the white flag, and yield.

I've found that it's a waste of time trying to force my will on others. I can lift my thoughts in prayer and focus on my desire to have peaceful relationships.

It is better to just let go and let God. When I've tried to impose my will on others, it has often ended in disaster. When I release my illusion of control, I receive God's power and I feel the Holy Spirit lift me in His love.

I want to be happy, joyous, and free. To do so, I let other people be seen, heard, and validated whether I agree or not. There is nothing wrong with us both being right.

Quote to Ponder

"Then Jesus said to His disciples, 'If anyone wishes to come after Me, he must deny himself, and take up his cross and follow Me. For whoever wishes to save his life will lose it; but whoever loses his life for My sake will find it'" (Matthew 16:24-25).

Take Action

Write, draw, pray, meditate, and reflect in ANEW's companion journal as follows:

Broken Feature:	Beautiful Feature:
Dear God, thank You for transforming the broken feature of YELLING into something beautiful.	Dear God, thank You for transforming the beautiful feature of YIELDING into something even more beautiful.

Questions beyond the introductory suggestions

- Was there yelling in my childhood home? What about my home now?
- Do I shake my fist at God or do I surrender to His gracious plan for my life?
- How can I yield my will to God's will for my life? For my loved ones' lives?
- With each new choice to yell or yield, can I ask myself, "How important will this be next year?"

❤️ CHAPTER 30 – Z FEATURES
Zero to Zenith

Dear God, thank You that I am transformed and made ANEW from the broken feature of ZERO with the beautiful feature of ZENITH by You.

For many years of my childhood and early adulthood, I felt worthless. I believed that it was my fault my mother drank and was unhappy. Why? That's what she told me. I thought I was defective because I wasn't able to fix her.

Soon, I began accepting blame for what went wrong in my mother's life. As a result of my misdirected guilt, I started taking on her household duties. This resulted in me becoming overly responsible and taking care of everyone's life around me. Since I was trying to play God, I failed to fix my mom's drinking and I was hurting myself. On a scale of one to ten, I felt like a zero.

I didn't know at the time that alcoholics blame everyone else, especially the people closest to them, for making them drink. That's not true; alcoholics drink because they have a disease.

Eventually, I found the Twelve Step communities of Alateen, Al-Anon, and Celebrate Recovery. These self-help groups taught me that alcoholism is a family disease, and I had been affected by it just with different symptoms than my mom. This discovery was a huge relief and a huge responsibility. I chose to take charge of my own life and spiritual awakening.

Through the rooms of Christian and self-help communities, I began a spiritual journey that led me to the foot of the cross and the arms of a Savior, the Lord Jesus Christ. I began to separate myself from my mom and live a separate life from her. This newfound freedom and faith in a loving God gave me the power and strength to raise my self-esteem from a zero to a zenith.

Something to Think About

My co-addiction sometimes shows itself in my quick defenses and explanations for what I say or don't say and do or don't do. I continue to grow and reach new heights in my self-esteem when I turn my will and life over to God and follow through on what I say I will do.

The Lord is on my side even when I forget. My spiritual practice reminds me of how much He has always been pursuing me. When I act like God, I keep His power out of my life and the lives of my loved ones. I remember that I lose when I fight His will.

God sees the broken and beautiful parts of my life and loves me still. Whether I have been in the valleys or on the mountaintops, He smiles on me. This knowledge gives me the freedom to reach new zeniths of growth and transformation.

My best is always good enough. I want to remember that God loves me as I am, and that transforms me.

Quote to Ponder

"For God did not give us a spirit of timidity, but a spirit of power, of love and of self-discipline" (2 Timothy 1:7).

Take Action

Write, draw, pray, meditate, and reflect in ANEW's companion journal as follows:

Broken Feature:	Beautiful Feature:
Dear God, thank You for transforming the broken feature of ZERO into something beautiful.	Dear God, thank You for transforming the beautiful feature of ZENITH into something even more beautiful.

Questions beyond the introductory suggestions

- Have I felt invisible or worthless? When and why?
- Do I know that God's love gives me the power to reach the heights of my potential?
- In what areas of my life can I surrender to the will, plan, and love of God to be raised up with Christ?
- When I'm in the valleys of my life, can I look up to the mountains knowing I will soon reach the top?

❤ 🤍 CHAPTER 31 – I AM ANEW
Features A to Z

Dear God, thank You that I am transformed and made ANEW from these A to Z broken features with beautiful ones by You.

With God, I AM ANEW from A to Z! This is a cause for celebration. Use this day to congratulate yourself on how much spiritual growth you have experienced by taking a balanced personal inventory.

- Do something fun to commemorate your accomplishment.
- Review your journal entries and add to your action plans for features from A to Z.
- Read the summary of features in this chapter and re-write them on the Blank I AM ANEW poster.
- Take time to pray and meditate on your journaling, the scriptures, and your action plans for the best time to make amends and offer forgiveness.

Lastly, consider spending the upcoming months re-reading the devotions and scriptures; go deeper by adding to your journal entries and action plans; and, take one action each day.

Quote to Ponder

"As the Father has loved me, so have I loved you. Now remain in my love...I have told you this so that my joy may be in you and that your joy may be complete" (John 15:9,11).

I AM ANEW from A to Z

God, in You, I AM ANEW from the broken feature of . . .	With the beautiful feature of . . .
A – Anger	A – Acceptance
B – Betrayal	B – Benevolence
C – Criticism	C – Compassion
D – Distracted	D – Disciplined
E – Envy	E – Empathy
F – Fearful	F – Forgiveness
G – Grief	G – Grateful
H – Helpless	H – Hopeful
I – Isolation	I – Intimacy
J – Judgment	J – Joyful
K – Killjoy	K – Kindness
L – Lonely	L – Loved
M – Misfit	M – Masterpiece

I AM ANEW from A to Z (continued)

God, in You, I AM ANEW from the broken feature of . . .	With the beautiful feature of . . .
N – Nervous	N – Nurturing
O – Opinionated	O – Open-Minded
P – Perfectionism	P – Prayerful
Q – Quarrelsome	Q – Quiet
R – Regret	R – Reverent
S – Shame	S – Self-Esteem
T – Thoughtless	T – Thoughtful
U – Uptight	U – Uplifting
V – Victim	V – Victorious
W – Willful	W – Willing
X – eXtreme	X – eXpressive
Y – Yelling	Y – Yielding
Z – Zero	Z – Zenith

94

REFERENCES

Baker, John. (2007). *Life's Healing Choices*. New York, NY: Howard Books.

Brown, Ph.D., MSW, Brené. (2013). *The Power of Vulnerability*. Narrated by Brené Brown. Louisville, CO: Sounds True Publishing. Audible audiobook.

Gibran, Kahlil. (1973). *The Prophet*. New York, NY: Alfred A. Knopf, Inc.

Habig, Cal. (2008, May 12). "Alan Redpath: Five Questions to Ask Before You Speak." [Blog Post]. Retrieved from http://talkingthewalk-cal.blogspot.com/2008/05/alan-redpath-five-questions-to-ask.html.

Kelly, Matthew. (2016). *Resisting Happiness*. Erlanger, KY: Beacon Publishing.

Niebuhr, Reinhold. (1934). "The Serenity Prayer." New York: NY: Union Theological Seminary.

Roper, David. (1994). *Psalm 23: The Song of a Passionate Heart*. Grand Rapids, MI: Discovery House Publishers.

Vujicic, Nick. (2013). *Life Without Limits*. New York, NY: WaterBrook Press.

Warren, Rick. (2002). *The Purpose Driven Life*. Grand Rapids, Michigan: Zondervan.

Weaver, K. D. (2018). *Meditate Like Jesus*. Eugene, OR: Wipf and Stock Publishers.

❤ ACKNOWLEDGMENTS

Special thanks to my family, church family, friends, mentors, editors, support partners, and sponsors in Al-Anon, Co-Dependent's Anonymous, and Celebrate Recovery, who inspired me and encouraged me to write this devotional.

Many thanks also to my coach, accountability partners, photo editor, and my special writing community, who helped me to polish and publish this devotional.

Above all, I am thankful for God's love for me in Jesus Christ that transforms the brokenness in my life daily into something beautiful.

💜 ABOUT THE AUTHOR

J. V. Lauren, P.E. combines nearly thirty years of technical writing expertise as a Professional Engineer with over thirty years of Bible study and self-help exploration to author the new Christian book set, *ANEW Spiritual Awakening*.

Her life is a testament to God's redeeming love. Her childhood and adult life were filled with neglect, loss, and abuse, including sexual abuse, which God has now healed. She overcame the pain of her parent's divorce, years of infertility, job losses, her divorce, raising twin boys, and the deaths of her mother, grandparents, and even her firstborn child.

She began her self-help journey while growing up in New England. Her mother's drinking brought her to the rooms of Al-Anon, Co-Dependents Anonymous, Celebrate Recovery, and open AA meetings. She learned she was not alone.

Working the Twelve Steps brought her to a saving faith in Jesus Christ. Since then, she continues to delve deeply into Twelve Step and scripture reading and application. She also completed an eight-year course with Bible Study Fellowship International.

She shares her experience, strength, and hope about how God transformed her brokenness into something beautiful. With God's help, her life is now filled with love, smiles, and laughter.

💙 WHAT NEXT?
What Do I Do Now?

Congratulations! You've finished an A to Z personal inventory using the *ANEW Spiritual Awakening: 31-Day Christian Devotional!*

If you haven't already done so, grab your copy of *ANEW Spiritual Awakening Companion Journal: 31-Day Christian Workbook* at https://www.amazon.com/dp/B08PFZ1DND.

Do you want more or need help to go deeper? We'd love for you to be a part of the ANEW community and work with our team!

Sign up at our website, www.anewwaynow.com, to view, print, or download the ANEW posters, if you haven't already! You will be notified of new books, upcoming masterclasses, workshops, and other resources.

Note that we will start filling spots for our upcoming masterclass early next year, so sign up fast when you get the notification!

Lastly, we will also send you links to uplifting merchandise for you and your loved ones for holidays, special occasions, or just for fun!

We look forward to serving you.

♥ CAN YOU HELP, PAW-LEASE?

Thank you for reading my book! I hope you loved it!

I need your help. Your review helps other people find this book and helps me make future versions better.

Please take two minutes now to leave me an honest review on Amazon letting me know what you thought of my book. Go to https://www.amazon.com/dp/B08PFDST59.

I appreciate all your feedback, and I enjoy hearing what you have to say.

Thanks so much!

J. V. Lauren